TRAPPED INSIDE MYSELF

AAKEEM WOODARD

Leadership Publishing

Dedications

I would like to thank Mrs. Collins; you believed in me when the world saw me as a monster. I'd also like to thank my trial Lawyer, David Wolf; my close friends Dennis Frances, Rev. Danny Horne, Arthur Hawkins, Pastor Mike Tedder and the Tabernacle staff, Pastor Marlin Harris, Pastor Mark Haston Rev. John Nash, Pastor Paul, and my close friend and brother in faith Pastor Aaron Antillon.

Thank you to Desiree Lee for pushing me to write this book. A special thanks to Steven Reba and Melisa Carter, who believed in me enough to fight for my freedom. Thank you to my parents and my grandmother, whom I call "mother" due to our strong bond. To my brothers and sisters, especially my little sister who loved me even though at times I did not deserve it. To Dr Robert Rohm for teaching me DISC and John Maxwell for writing into my life I say keep changing the world.

A special thanks also goes to my wife, Pamela, whom I love and cherish, and who gave me the joy of my life: my two sons, Josiah Isaiah Woodard and Jordon Emanuel Woodard. They will be better than me, stronger than me, and wiser than me.

Table of Contents

Words of Wisdom

There comes a time in life when you have had enough, and your spirit begins to place pressure on your mind to change.

There I was a high school dropout, at odds with myself and lost in the same darkness that has engulfed so many of our youth today. At the age of sixteen, instead of enjoying the best years of my life by getting my learner's license or having a girlfriend, I was in court being tried as an adult. Even though I was still a child, I was being tried as an adult for taking a life during an armed robbery. My life had no meaning, no feelings, no hope, no aspirations, no dreams, and no light to see my way out of the darkness that embraced me. It was only by the grace of God—who put people in my life who would push me to become the person God created me to be—that I found that light that guided me out of darkness. As my life changed, I left bread crumbs along the way, signs that would become a road map for others to follow. I never knew that one day I would have to go back into that darkness, following my own bread crumbs in order to save our youth.

Trapped Inside Myself

The one thing about prison that you need to know is don't believe everything you hear. It's the things you don't hear that you should be concerned about.

As I looked out over the yard at the lost young faces, it struck me how so many of them seemed happy, laughing and playing as if they were at home. Prison to us had become a way of life, a home away from home. I began to wonder if this could be all that life had become for us. Could we truly feel comfortable being locked away from our family and separated from society? Some of the guys in prison were locked up with half the guys from their neighborhoods, guys they grew up with. To them a day in prison was like being with family. They spent most of the day talking about different events they had shared in life. It was as if we had learned how to mask our pain by finding other destructive things to do. Robbing each other, lying to each other, fighting each other, and sometimes killing each other were normal day-to-day activities in prison.

One of the most destructive things was our lack of awareness about the importance of time. Being sentenced to five years or ten years had no effect on the minds of these young men, including me. Prison had become a right of passage, a norm among a whole generation. You were a nobody in the streets unless you had served time in prison. If you were the one who had been released from prison but came back and now were being released again, you were above the law in the prison's eyes—even though you had spent over a decade in and out of prison.

I looked at myself in the mirror and hated the man that I had become. I saw someone who had yet to feel the weight of a life lost due to my hands. I asked myself, "Is this the reason God brought me into this world? Is my life meant to be nothing but pain and darkness?" But my life had to have meaning, a purpose beyond these walls. How could I change the negative impact that I'd had on my life and on the lives of others? It was only when I embraced the pain and the hurt I had caused others that remorse became action.

You see, it means nothing to say that you are sorry when those words don't produce any actions to change. Only in your actions can you see the truth about your statements of remorse. True remorse demands action. Without actions, they are baseless words. Positive change and meaningful actions show a genuine apology and a readiness to actively avoid making the same bad choices.

God showed me that the same hands that took a life can and will save many lives. Through my struggle I can and will give hope to that young lost soul and provide a tool for that lost parent. So, with my life, I give to you a road map that will offer a different outlook on our young adults who are in the judicial system, those who are fighting to stay out of it, and those who seem to wish to return. Those who don't believe in the power of God will see the power of His will and the timing of His wisdom. This book is written to change our lives and be-gin to be responsible and accountable to everyone and every system that is involved with trying to raise a child in this world. Welcome to Relentless.

CHAPTER ONE

A Lonely Place

Every teen who sits in a courtroom realizes that the way things should have happened in court was only in their minds. Reality won't stop playing through your mind. As you are given your sentence and moved away from the eyes of your family, the sound of doors closing behind you is something you will never get used to. To go from having the choice of when to eat, what to eat, or how you would like to have it cooked to eating only what they give you can and will destroy you from the inside out. It can make you bitter at the world while eating away at your soul, if you allow it. It took many years for me to learn that freedom is a choice.

However, giving in to it (and I will explain what that "it" is) is why so many men come home from prison bitter and angry at the world. They treat their family and friends as if they owe them something. You become this selfish creature who cares nothing about anyone else; an inner disease eats you up from the inside out. By the time it starts to spread to other parts of your thinking, the host is already dead—walking, talking, and eating but dead.

I was going to a youth development center tried as an adult for a crime committed at the age of fifteen. Fear gripped my soul; confusion ran through my mind like the blood in my veins. But I would show no fear. My life was full of so many dark moments that I had convinced myself to believe that it was better for me to be in the dark. I felt that this was the only way to be free in my world—to become a creature of the dark so no one could see that this little boy was afraid and ready to go home. The judge's words vibrated through my body repeatedly, words I would never forget, words that would haunt me for many years to come. Judge Huff told me to stand, and he sentenced me to prison for the rest of my life for felony murder and armed robbery. My mother fell to the floor, and people shouted. I just kept telling myself that in a few months things would change, and I would be free to go home, that somehow my lawyer would pick me up and take me home.

How did my life become so dark? How did I become so lost, so far away from the path to success? Every snowball that starts small, the more it rolls, the bigger it gets. So was my life. The minor misbehavior, the desire to be liked, my attitude toward life—these things that I was going through never stopped and were never truly addressed. Now, even if I wanted to stop it, the ball had become too big and too fast for me to do so.

Let's back up because my life did not start like this. I come from a two-parent home, where both parents are college graduates. Because of my parents' interpretation of the Jehovah Witnesses' religion, which they followed, we were not allowed to play sports. We were told that sports and competition were tools of the devil. I never really formed a relationship with God. To me He had more rules than my parents did. People around me were being kicked out of the Witnesses organization for their sins. As we were told by my parents, the world would end soon so there was no need to dream about a true future. I hated this God and the faith that promoted these beliefs. Track was my outlet; it was my passion. But to my parents it was a sin. I was born in Albany, Georgia. My mother received a higher-paying job at Southern Bell at the same time my father's place of employment closed down, so we moved to Atlanta, and, subsequently, my life began to unravel. Albany had been slow, but Atlanta was moving extremely fast. The city gave my mind few chances to rest before being confronted with the next issue. It was like a constant high.

Parents don't fully understand the emotional war that goes on inside a child when you just pack up and leave everything you know of life to go off into the unknown. Parents look at it as a new start, but a child doesn't have the same capacity to start over. How can you start over when you are so connected to everything and everyone around you? The move for me was like a crushing of memories. Moments of happiness were followed by days of sadness. Against my parents' beliefs, I started to run track at Norcross High School. When I ran, I felt so alive it didn't matter that my grades were not as high as others'. All that mattered was that, with the wind behind me, I was free, free from all the mistakes of my past. I can remember running home with a first-place trophy for track-and-field day. I was so excited! Track was something I was good at. I rushed into the house to show my mother. I said, "Look, Mama! Look! I may not be as smart as my sisters, but I won first place!" My mother didn't even look at it or me. She only said, "You know what God says about competition." *A chain in me broke.*

The next day I was out walking with some friends. As we were walking, I found myself going over to some random guy. I just walked up to this guy, who was getting into his car, and I knocked him out from behind for nothing more than to get a laugh from my friends. I felt nothing about how that man felt. I did not feel empathy for my actions. I did not think if he had a wife or kids. Anger and frustration fueled my actions. My friends recognized me for my actions, even said I was without fear. To them I was somebody; to them I was real. The anger that I felt and the feeling of loss, created by the lack of acknowledgment from my parents and other factors of growing up, became like a disease eating me from inside. *Another chain in me broke.* The chain that held the human side of me together.

Over the next year, sports were slowly being replaced with destructive behavior and fast money. I started leaving home, running away for a day or two. I can remember coming home after being gone for a few days. I opened the door to see my mother in tears. She placed her hands on my shoulders and asked me, "What is wrong with you? Why do you hurt me in such a way?" If you had asked me if I would ever hurt my mother or father, I would be the first to say no; I would protect them with my life. However, my life was owned by the streets, driven by the acceptance and power that the streets had to offer. I didn't care about what would come as a result of my actions down the line; I lived for the second. So I could not see that I was on a path that only had two ways out: death or prison.

My parents had rules, but the streets had none. That so-called freedom was attractive to me. A lot of my friends' parents allowed them to do anything, even smoke in front of them. Don't get me wrong; I love my parents. However, their rules made me feel like they never saw my pain or heard my cry to be known in an unknown world. I felt like I lacked a voice. I screamed inside to be free of the pain of being told who or what to do while no one seemed to care about what Aakeem would like to do. My parents' answer to a problem was a spanking. After so many years of that, I became numb to that form of punishment. I would only cry so my parents would think they had hurt me, and they would stop. Our family looked so good on the outside, and we were praised by many. But, on the inside, we were going through so many dark things.

I started stealing cars with a few friends when we were recruited by men old enough to be our fathers. They would pay us well below what we should have received for those cars. We were all below the age of sixteen, so our driving skills were not perfect. We would steal about ten cars off of the lot and wreck about two. We would lose two more when the police chased us. So we only brought six cars when we were told to bring ten and didn't get all the money we were promised. Just when I thought that I could make a life out of stealing cars, a shift happened again in my life. I was bused out to Parkview High School; at that time in 1987–88, I was the only black boy at the school.

On my first day, I saw the only black girl there. I walked over to her to introduce myself, but she looked at me as if I was Jason from *Friday the 13th*. You know that look of horror as if to say, "My God, where did he come from? He must have come to kill me." What was I doing in this school trying to fit in where I didn't want to fit in? In class, I remember trying to answer a question. My hand was raised yet the teacher kept looking over me. Someone yelled out, "The only reason he is in this school is they want him to play football!" The class laughed along with the teacher. I could see the hatred in her face for me just being there. That was the last time I tried to speak in any class, ever. *Another chain broke.*

You can call it whatever you want to call it, but white kids who have never been around black kids truly believe that we all act like what they see on the videos. People say that white kids want to be black or try to act black. I say that's a lie. What person would choose to be at a disadvantage in life and always have to fight for their rights? Some black kids live in areas where a young white male would never drive, and, at the same time, black males fill up the prisons by the thousands. So please don't flatter yourself. They don't want to be black. My white classmates were drawn to a lifestyle that they saw on TV. So it should not be a surprise that to gain friends I became that guy in the video— the one who didn't care about school. I became that gangster. The more out of control I was, the more friends I made.

This caught the attention of one guy that I should have run away from. His name was Thomas. His mom let him do anything. I thought it was cool being able to smoke and drink in front of your mom. A friend of Thomas's named Dana, who would become my codefendant, and I looked up to Thomas. I begin to tell false stories about committing harsh crimes and evading the law, which really impressed him. Thomas was that guy your parents would tell you to stay away from. However, we envied the freedom that his parents gave him. One day Thomas came up with a plan to rob a store. He said that we would get paid and that he and Dana had already looked the place over. I was a duck (a person who would follow someone into a fire and not question why we were burning). It's the loyalty to a system of crime that cares nothing about us. Most kids won't admit they are ducks, followers, but most kids who get into trouble are simply ducks. I was a follower who wanted to impress this guy so badly that I didn't say anything when the plan meant that I had to go in with a gun. That desire to be accepted sometimes becomes more important than air.

This situation is not uncommon. Most teens who end up involved in serious crimes are not the leaders of the pack. They are the followers. Kids are the victims of their own uncontrolled desire to fit in. I sold drugs, stole cars, and even ran out of stores with merchandise. Even I couldn't explain why I was so willing to rob a store. The snowball had started to grow out of control. On the night the plan was to take place, I begged my mom to let me go over to a friend's house. I was trying anything to get away from the situation. It was something yelling inside me to get away so when the guys came for me, I would not be at home. My mom once again said no. Even my father said no. I knew then that I would not get away from this plan to rob that store. I felt trapped. Too often when kids are trying to ask for help, parents don't pick up on the language. Communication with youth is not just about words. It's a touch, an acknowledgment, a sacrifice, or just seeing your children for who they are instead of who you want them to be

You may say, "Well, you could have just walked away." Yes, I could have if I owned enough of myself to say no. But that is not how I felt at fifteen. That night Thomas and Dana came to get me. I was only fifteen years old in ninth grade. They were older than me so they could drive. I still think, "God, why did I sneak out of the house that night!"

Because it was the end of my life as it had been. Dana and I were told that no one would get hurt. In that situation, having such little life experience, you want to believe that no one will get hurt. A kid wants to convince him- or herself that it's not that big of a deal and everything will be all right. I've come to know that when you put a gun in your hand, you cannot control the outcome—and on top of that, that no one goes into a crime thinking they will get caught.

We never spoke about hurting anyone. My heart was pounding, and my mind was telling me to stop, but my legs kept moving toward the store. I felt panicky, but I also felt like I had no options. When I look back, I wonder if it was the drugs Dana and I smoked with Thomas before he sent us on this mission. Or was it the overwhelming emotional prison of wanting to fit in that would not allow me to just walk away? I truly believe it was both forces pushing me forward. That night, while robbing that store, I took a life that I had no right to take. In that one second, I ended my life as well. The ride back to my house seemed like forever. I crawled back into my bed with my ears ringing from the gunshot. My last thought was "What have I done?" I wanted to close my eyes, hoping this was all a bad dream. The thump, thump of my heart was like dynamite in my ears. Then the drugs begin to calm me down, and a sense of invisibility washed over me.

Wrapped in this feeling of power is what I woke up to the next morning. The magnitude of my actions didn't have the space in my chest to grow. I was still processing life on a child's level. I could not free myself from the gun as if it was controlling me. I saw in *The Lord of the Rings* how crazy Gollum was for the ring he called Precious. It reminded me so much of how that gun had become my Precious. I pointed it at people, and they would submit. I had become the gangster in the movies but a lost soul to me and others.

I still can remember the morning the police came into my house. They arrived in large numbers and suddenly pulled me out of my bed. My mother was crying and asking what was going on. The look in her eyes said it all. For the first time, I saw her lost and unable to help her son. It was as if a light went out inside of her. My little sister was holding on to my leg and kept asking me why they were taking me. I felt as if the air had been sucked out of my lungs. I could feel and hear my heart pounding. The impact of what I had done still had not hit me like it should have. It was the fear of being caught that was pulling me down.

I loved my parents, but we never could talk. Now I had placed myself into a position that nobody could get me out of, and I needed to communicate with them more than before. Yet I am grateful that the police came to get me that morning. It had been seven days since the crime. An entire week had gone by, and I had caught that juice. You know that juice. Remember the movie *Juice* with Tupac, who plays Bishop? After robbing a store and shooting the clerk, Bishop allows the gun to fill him up with a false since of power. He becomes out of control. It's hard to explain how that gun in my hand made me feel. It was as if I possessed the power to make people respect me. I suddenly felt I had control in a world where my life always felt out of control. I was lost in that immense power. It became my high, my addiction. I can remember going into a party full of adults, and when someone pushed up on me, all I had to do was show that gun and they would back down. *Another chain broke.*

I was only sixteen years old when I sat in the courtroom. I was being tried as an adult for armed robbery and felony murder. I was zero help to my lawyer. Instead of telling him the truth and giving him the tools he needed to defend me, I continued to lie to my lawyer and my family. I denied that I had done anything wrong. I was afraid that if my mom knew the truth, I would lose her love and support. I thought I would even lose my lawyer's assistance, and he would no longer fight for my freedom if he knew what I had done.

The magnitude of what I had done had not yet filled my soul. As I grew up behind those walls, the understanding of life made me see just how much pain I had caused so many people. All that I could see at the time was that my mom was paying all my legal fees. None of those friends I had in and out of school came to my aid or helped my mom with the money for the lawyer. When you are young, you think that your friends will be there for you and that they have your back no matter what. Your friends are your family and your support network as a kid. Sometimes your friends feel like your entire world. I promise you this: that talk about "ride or die" or "I have your back" is a joke. They will move on with their lives. Some may even say you went out bad and make you the object of the joke for many years to come. They go on with their lives—school, work, family—and forget about you. Your friends are not obligated to keep you on their minds. You die to them before you spend a year in prison, while your nightmare has just begun.

It seemed so strange to me that when I looked behind me in court, I would always see the one person to whom I had given the hardest of times—the one person I had disobeyed and fought against the most, that one person who had sacrificed the most for me. That person was my mother. She swore no allegiance to any colors or flags. She stood only for the love of her son—a love that I never understood how to give her in return. My love was for the streets. I had love for a place that never loved me in return. The streets had no rules while my mother had many. The streets didn't care if I had good grades in school or that I even went to school. It was my parents who cared about those things.

My father was a part of my life, but we never took the time to know one another. He was always working to take care of us. It was only after many years of prison that I found out that my father was a in one of the well-known college Greek fraternities the Omega Psi Phi. I wish he had told me about his past and how he grew up, so that I could say I wanted to pledge like my dad. In Albany, I would sneak out to the college to watch the Q-dogs step. You should have seen me; I had every step down. I never saw my dad as someone out there stepping. There were even great things about my mom that she never talked about like marching with Rev. Martin Luther King Jr. Why did they keep these things from me? The Jehovah Witnesses' faith made them hate their past in such a way that even the inspiring things became sins. Because they didn't believe in those things now should not have kept them from giving us the chance to know who they were. Most parents work to shield their kids from the mistakes of their past and even the hardship of the present. When parents get mad at their children's inappropriate actions and call them ungrateful, it's not that the kids are ungrateful; it's because parents don't tell their children about the struggle to make it day by day. They don't share those moments in time when it takes all that they've got to get through the day. When they ate, it was because of the sacrifices the parents made. All they see is new clothes, new shoes, and a refrigerator full of food. Youth need to understand the fight that parents go through every day so they can have nice things. They need to understand the process.

All this didn't matter now. In court, they used so many terms that I was not familiar with, and I couldn't even make a guess about what they meant for me in my situation. I was being treated as an adult even though everyone in the courtroom knew I was still a child. I wasn't even old enough to drive or drink. Society thought I was too immature to vote, get married, or buy a beer, but here I was being charged as an adult. I was treated like an adult and expected to understand the adult judicial system.

The judge gave me a life sentence for my actions. His words echoed through my soul: "I sentence you to prison for the rest of your life." Dana received the same sentence due to my actions, and Thomas walked free. I had only lived on this earth for a short while and managed to place myself in a position that robbed me of my future. At the time, I couldn't grasp the magnitude of my actions. It was far too big for my small mind to take in. I was going to a youth development center, and when I turned seventeen, I would be sent to prison with a life sentence. A sentence like that is nearly impossible for a child to understand. I kept thinking that my lawyer would find a way to get me out of this. I couldn't spend the rest of my life in this place away from home. All this would come to an end, and I would go home. I had to go home. I wanted things in my life, but I didn't understand the process in this instant world.

I can still see those young men who came into the youth development center with nonviolent crimes only to be educated on how to do more elaborate and violent crimes. They learned how to plan a home invasion, how to pull off a robbery, and even how to get rid of a body. Most of those young men left with big ideas on how to do bolder crimes. These stories on how to make money through drugs, scams, and forgery had me wrapped up and ready to try one out. I kept planning in my mind and thinking over possibilities on how I could commit these crimes. If I had made bond, I'm sure that I would have committed more crimes. I had become a product of the juvenile system. I had no faith and no relationship with God. My vision for my life became the crimes of others.

Parents think that if their child goes away to a youth development center for a while it will have a positive impact on his or her life. They will learn their lesson. Yes, they will learn a lesson, and not just lessons on the topics parents are expecting. They will master subjects that parents would cringe to hear about and, consequently, not learn the lessons they had hoped for in court when they received their sentences.

CHAPTER TWO

An Emotional Time Bomb

In juvenile, we fought a lot trying to prove who was the meanest or toughest. To tell the truth, I believe we were all afraid—afraid to be ourselves, afraid to laugh, afraid to be a kid. It was as if being a child was being weak. The paths we had chosen made us grow up before our time. There would be times when, for a few minutes, we would laugh and play. Then a fight would break out, and we were quickly reminded that we were not free. Even though we were children, we had left childhood behind. Being a silly kid was forbidden. It was a weakness that had to die in us if we were going to survive in this place. Those little moments of laughter though are what I remember the most over the many crazy things that I experienced. To survive, I lost what little I owned of myself in the lifestyle of incarceration. *The last chain that held me to being human broke.*

I remember that some of the female staff in Milledgeville Youth Development Center started to do nice things for some of us—a touch on the shoulder, a breast rubbed up against us, or a hard stare followed by a seductive smile. One time, a female staff member who had been particularly nice to me asked if I would like to kiss her. Of course, I had been dreaming of this moment ever since she started touching me and talking to me. That day we held each other close and kissed. I was in love the moment that our lips touched. I left society having very limited experience with females. Now, here I was with a grown lady, and she loved me. Hiding behind that love I felt, I no longer could see the wired fence that had become my home. Being locked away started to not be so bad. I wore my emotions like a suit of armor. Little did I know that I was only strapping an emotional bomb around my waist that would soon explode.

My actions led me unexpectedly into a whole new world of young boys, female staff, and sex. The underground sex club that I was now a member of was overwhelming. It was a privilege to go back to the dorm with a female to have sex while other staffers looked out for you. After the female you had sex with left the dorm, you could see other female staff waiting for their turn with their young man. We felt special as if we were in a class above the rest. We worshipped these females. Little did we know, we were only being used to fill the sexual void for these women who were not getting any attention at home. At that time, we didn't see it for what it truly was: child abuse. If we were questioned about our dealings with those females, none of us would say that we were having sex. Why would we cut off the only thing that made us feel alive?

I thought that I was really in love. I felt I was loved, that I was truly in a loving relationship, until I found out that I was not the only one. The female employees were enjoying more than just one young man at this camp, and our emotions meant nothing to them. They didn't love us, nor were they going to live up to the promises of being with us when we went home. Some females were having a relationship with up to three young men at the same time. All of the youth at the facility desired to be accepted by someone. We needed it more than we needed money. It is crazy that when we were in the streets, we craved money over being loved, but being locked up changed that. To tell the truth, I believe that chasing money was just something to hide behind due to the lack of love in our lives. The world had given up on us, and society was afraid of us. In that darkness, the feeling of love was our only light. No one had the right to play with our emotions. We were the outcasts, the ones that society had to lock away in a cage. To use us the way we were being used meant nothing to the female staff.

To watch young men in tears or feeling sad because a female said she had found another man or that the young man was too childish for her created an emotional vacuum of hate. We willingly allowed ourselves to be pulled into that hate. It shielded us from the pain. When I asked the female I was in love with if I was the only one in her life, she said that I was special and that she was enough woman for me and others to share. I couldn't go for that. It was devastating for a teenage boy in my circumstances. I told her that I should be the only one. The next day she told me that she had found someone else who was more mature than me. She said I had blown my chance to be with her again. This was the first time a female broke my heart.

Disappointment, sadness, anger, betrayal, and frustration were all emotions no one had taught me how to handle. That same longing for acceptance that led me, and many of the youth, to be in a juvenile detention facility was once again being used against me. My misguided emotions became a fire that burned me up from the inside. I became even more angry at the world and, consequently, less angry at myself for my own actions. It created a vicious cycle.

It's not always the youth who are in the wrong when you find them jumping on staff. Many of the young men who hit the staff or spit on female guards during those years had been emotionally hurt by them. We were used as emotional doormats by those who cared nothing about us. Many of these young men went on with their lives emotionally scarred, which often gave birth to abusive behavior toward females.

When we acted out because of that anger, the staff took us to the hole. The hole is a small cell with a slab of concrete to sleep on. Once the door is closed, it has a small flap for getting your food tray. When you came in yelling about how you had been done wrong, the staff would send the nurse to see you. My first time meeting with the nurse was something I never wish on anyone. They came into my cell because I was beating on the cell door. They held me down, and the nurse gave me a shot that locked up my body. All I could do was move my eyes. I couldn't even stop from urinating on myself. We called the shot "hound dog." Looking back, I realize that we were being treated wrong in so many ways. We were seen as nothing but objects. My heart became even darker.

I commend the Georgia Department of Juvenile Justice for its hard work in protecting the youth. Commissioner Avery D. Niles, along with our governor Nathan Deal, sincerely fought hard to change the culture within the system. Their efforts have saved lives inside and outside the facilities. Parents and other departments should join in these historic moves to keep the youth in these facilities safe. However, this was in 1989, and you can only imagine how many young men were affected by this type of treatment.

CHAPTER THREE

Someone Who Cares

The juvenile detention center had become my home and a new type of school for me where I was taught countless ways to commit crimes. As I walked between the buildings of the facility, I felt a hand on my shoulder. I turned around to see this little lady staring up at me. The first thought that came to my sixteen-year-old mind was "It's the little lady in the movie *Poltergeist*," followed by my second thought, "Run to the light, Carol Anne."

She looked me in the eyes and said, "Each day I have watched you just throw your life away. If you keep going down this path that you have chosen for your life, you will be dead long before your time, and if they let you out, you will come right back. I'm here because I care."

I immediately yelled at her with all the fear and pain I had inside of me. "They gave me a life sentence. You know what that means? It means that my life is already over. Why do you even care?"

She didn't even flinch while still looking into my eyes. She said words that I will never forget. She said, "Because God cares about you." This woman went on to tell me that she was not going to sit back and let me throw my life away. As she walked away, she stated matter-of-factly that she would see me at the library the following day.

All that night I tried to convince myself that no one was going to tell me what to do. But I couldn't get her words out of my head. I even thought about being sick as an excuse not to go. The next day I found myself walking into the library, and there stood Mrs. Collins. It was as if she was waiting for me. She asked me what my hopes and dreams were, adding value to my life when I was at a loss for words. Looking up to me, she held my hand and said, "No matter how far you think that you have fallen, you still have the power to get back up." My toughness broke. The fog created by my fear began to lift. Mrs. Collins was like a mother to me; she mentored me like a son.

By working with her, I developed the desire to learn. I constantly tried to educate myself. I was always looking for a way to free my mind from the pressures of others around me. It was as if a light had been turned on. I could see the world yielding its knowledge to those who looked for it. One thing that the staff, counselors, wardens, and even officers need to know is that when you're young, you can tell when an adult is really trying to help you or a person truly cares about you. Mrs. Collins knew the crime I had committed, and despite my actions, she still chose to care about me. Now that was powerful. I asked her once why she was so nice to me. She said, "God does not give me the right not to love you." She was my first encounter with true Christianity. It wasn't the Bible-thumping, "you're going to go to hell if you don't change your ways" kind of religion or the Jehovah Witnesses' way of turning their backs on you when you are exiled from their religion. It was the gospel, the love of God showed through this little lady, whom I called Momma. Little did I know that the seeds she planted would take over a decade to grow. You know what? I truly believe she was OK with the timing of God.

Soon, with her guidance, I was able to receive my GED and start college, but my road to rehabilitation came to an end on my seventeenth birthday. I had hoped this day would never come, that by some miracle I would be allowed to do most of my time at the juvenile facility. Nonetheless, when I turned seventeen, a bus pulled up to the youth center to transport me to the adult prison. The night before, my heart was pounding. I was about to move away from the people who had become my family. No one prepared me for what I was about to face. No one educated me on what to do and how to do it, or what not to do. Like all of the youth today who are tried as adults, I was hung over a pot of fire when I turned seventeen. As kids are dropped into this pot, they are told not to get burned. Very few are able to survive with their minds intact. All of us who came to adult prison by way of being tried as an adult were damaged in some way or another. Mrs. Collins could not prepare me for something that she had never experienced. I can remember that she said, with tears in her eyes, "Never forget who loves you." Fear strangled the little light that had started to shine within me. I needed more time with those who cared about me. I had to realize the hard way that change doesn't come easy, or on our time.

CHAPTER FOUR

Going to Hell on Earth

As I approached the prison, I could see the rows of barbed wire that looked like a sea of razors. I would be lying if I said that I was not afraid. My heart pounded, but I knew I couldn't show any fear. I could see the guns in the officers' hands. The looks on their faces told me just how much they hated us. I wasn't asked how I wanted my hair to be cut. It was just cut like everyone else's: a two-minute bald cut. Before we were allowed into the population, we were told that the doctor would be checking all of us for prostate cancer. If we didn't allow him to do a finger probe, we would be locked down.

Yes, this was the sexual sickness in Alto State Prison at that time. Check the records; check the staff. Everyone knew what was going on. This practice was never done anywhere else. Prisons don't even search for contraband in that manner. This barbaric action was done in Alto State Prison in Georgia during the 1980s and 90s. There was no need for such a check because we were under twenty-five years old. Even the officers and nurses were aware of what this doctor was doing to us, and nobody tried to stop him. Even though it was a one-time action, you never forgot it. By law there must be a reason for such a search, not just a requirement that all prisoners who come to Alto State Prison have this type of cavity search. I tell young men today that when your actions put you in a place like prison, you don't know what you will be made to do or how your life will forever be touched.

Once my head was shaved, we were sprayed down for lice, and then we put on our jumpsuits. My heart was pounding. As our group of new intakes was paraded around the camp, I could hear people yelling. In the early 1990s, Alto State Prison was out of control. Every day someone was stabbed or raped. A life had no value. Someone would stab or rob you for a ten-cent soup. Going to the officers for help was like talking to a wall. Unlike in juvenile, these officers could care less about how you survived. The officers were only concern with one thing which was how to get back home safely. If it took allowing a prisoner to be beaten or taken advantage of for them to finish a day safely. then we were out of luck. We were all on our own. My life could have been taken at any moment. An African American asking for help would only make the officers laugh and cause him to gain even more enemies. Eighty percent of the white population was in protected custody— some had been there for years—while 10 percent were in the mental health dorms. The rest of us were packed in like crabs in a bucket.

I remember a young man around eighteen who was beaten badly and sexually assaulted and left in the bathroom. Because he was from a small town that had few people in prison, he had very little protection. (It was all about what county you were from or if you were from Atlanta or down south.) To the officers it was a joke. After the young man tried to explain to them what had happened, their words to him were "you should have stayed at home." As I watched other dark things go on around me, my heart became darker. I became a product of a criminal environment. Like I said before, I didn't own enough of myself to say no to those destructive behaviors. Before I could become a victim of a robbery or even be killed in prison, I started to rob, steal, fight, and gamble. I felt that I had to become a monster so I wouldn't be eaten by the monsters living around me.

In the juvenile detention center, at least they pushed education. In prison, education was a joke. The education was there, but it was the desire to take part in it that was the joke. To fight against the negative current in prison you had to be self-motivated. And this is a tool that 90 percent of those in prison don't have—a tool that at that time in my life I knew I didn't have. I dehumanized myself because humans didn't survive in a place like this. Only a wild beast could live in a land of wild animals. So I became that wild animal, void of emotion, lost in a jungle of my own thoughts. In that steel hell, having feelings for others would get you killed.

The Department of Corrections continues to create programs that it feels will help people return to society. The programs attempt to prepare inmates to be helpful instead of harmful to society. However, the program results are rarely seen. It's not that the tools for education are not there; it's the will to make a change or the vision to see the end of transformation that's not there. All that you can see is how to make it through another day trapped in the steel jungle of your mind. How can you help someone who feels he doesn't need help? How can you help me to understand that I need a skill when I have ten more years to do in prison? How can you tell someone in prison to stop selling drugs when he is making more money selling drugs in prison than he was making in society? There was an underlying tone in prison that education was for the weak ones. And it was me and others who were the weak ones. We were afraid to show that we were willing to change or that we regretted our actions. How far I had fallen from the person I was when I was with Mrs. Collins in juvenile. I was trapped inside of myself—a prison far greater than the one I was standing in.

Alto State Prison became my home. To bury the pain of not going home, the prison became me, and I became the prison. I can remember talking on the phone to my little brother, telling him how cool prison was and how we were making money pushing drugs and staying high most of the day. How I wish I could have told him the harsh, true reality of prison. My words caused my little brother to want to be like me, and like me he also ended up in prison for shooting someone. (My next book will address generational curses.) My mind was so far into dark places that I can honestly say if I had made parole during my first seven years in prison, I would have committed more crimes. All I wanted to do was get out, push crack, get a nice car, and spend money. Some of the young drug dealers in Alto had the pictures and money to back up their stories. I had nothing to show for what brought me to prison. I lived through their stories, each day dreaming about being a true drug dealer.

I had lost myself in the darkness that was alive all around me. I was not strong enough to be a leader. I didn't own enough of myself to say no to the evil things going on around me. If you don't own yourself, then rest assured, *someone else owns you.*

Even the smell of prison was different. And the pressure to survive was more intense. The darkness that hung over and stills hangs over prisons can be felt the moment you walk into these places. The cycle that so many young men were on at that time was incredible. A guy would go home. We would talk to him on the phone. And within six months he was either dead or back in prison. No one complained about coming back. It was like a game of tag that everybody was playing with the system. With each year I became a brick in the prison wall. These thoughts, along with the loss of hope and the crazy things going on around me, were too much. I dropped out of college, losing the means for an education, only to gain so-called friends that I would soon learn meant me no good.

CHAPTER FIVE

Mothers

My mother was a great help in showing me just how far I had fallen from being the son that she held in her arms. I had allowed my mistake at the age of fifteen to take my life into utter darkness. By this time, my mother and father were divorced and not even speaking to each other. My father told me that being a man was about accepting the consequences that result from your actions. That was when I finally told him that I did do that senseless crime and took a life that I had no right to take. He told me that he always knew that, but he needed me to tell him so I could begin to accept my punishment for my actions.

After seven years of lying to my mom about not committing my crime, I broke down and told her the truth. She was upset and angry, but she didn't stop loving me. She asked me to look at my life, to look at the years that I had spent in prison, and ask myself, "What have I done to better myself?" She stood up during visitation and said, "I will come see you, support you, and write you only when you decide that you will seek to better yourself—to become the son I can be proud of and others can too." Then she got up and left without looking back. She left me sitting there with that statement running through my head.

Later that week, I received a letter from Mrs. Collins. She said, "I have come to know that you have lost your way inside that prison. You should open your eyes and do not look outward. You must look inward to find your way back to that bright young man that I have come to love as a son. Fight, fight with all that you've got in order to find your way back home." That night, when I looked at myself in the mirror, I did not recognize the person looking back at me. I had already fallen into the same routine of mistakes that had led me to prison. I knew I had to change, but the question was how. There was no one teaching us how to reinvent ourselves. The counselors were so busy that all you had to do was show up at a self-help class on corrective thinking, victim impact, or family violence, and you would pass.

CHAPTER SIX

Looking for a Place to Belong

I looked around me and saw that the strongest people behind those walls were the Muslims. Not physically but mentally. They would challenge the wildest guy in the dorm with wisdom, not muscle. At that time the Muslims were truly reforming the boys into men. Let me get rid of a myth: everyone in prison becomes religious. It is simply not true. Not everyone going to prison becomes a Muslim or a Christian. In every prison that I have been, both groups put together were still in the minority. If you had one thousand people in a prison, at the most, 160 to two hundred were involved in religious services on any level, with the Muslims being the smaller population of the two religions. I was hungry for change; however, I was caught up in so many negative things, such as drugs, smoking cigarettes, and gambling, that I didn't believe I could change.

I continued to watch how the Muslims lived their lives. They were always reading, writing, studying, or praying. A young brother named Abdulla must have seen me watching because he invited me to read the Holy Quran with him. I was ashamed to be seen reading with the Muslims because it meant you were leaving your old ways behind, and that included old friends. I only read the Quran when no one was around. I was ashamed about getting my life together. But Brother

Abdulla was patient with me. He understood that the more I invested in me, the further away from my old friends I would become. When I decided to become a Muslim, that day I gave up everything—smoking drugs, gambling, stealing, and fighting over nothing. I spent most of my days studying the Islamic faith to build my character. The leader in me started to awaken. I didn't desire to be a Muslim who sat and just followed. I was tired of being a duck, a follower. God was pushing me to be what He created me to be: a leader.

I didn't have to fight to get away from old friends. I didn't have to fight to get away from old habits. I had outgrown them. I needed to learn all I could, so I started to take multiple steps in that direction. I repeated all the self-help classes that I had taken before. This time I didn't care about a certificate; I was taking these classes to better myself. I kept up with current events locally and internationally. While others were asleep, I read books like *Rich Dad Poor Dad, The Art of War,* and *Seven Habits of Highly Effective People*, as well as American history and Islamic history. While I used to get up in the morning and listen to rap music, I now started listening to NPR news. For a year I didn't watch TV, listen to music, or even talk a lot. It was time to listen and learn. I had become detached from the inner workings of prison. It was time for me to escape the mental pull of prison. I found a torn book in the library that was a big part of saving my life. It was John Maxwell's *21 Irrefutable Laws of Leadership*. Maxwell's teachings on leadership allowed me to grow bigger than being just a person with a number on my back. It was a book that would change my life forever.

CHAPTER SEVEN

A New Reality

When I finally took the time to catch my breath, I realized that I had escaped prison. My mind had found a way to jump the fence and was waiting for my body to catch up. I started to care about people. I wanted them to be able to taste the freedom that I was experiencing. Therefore, I decided to start teaching others how to escape prison, which is a task that many guys in prison are afraid to even begin. To teach guys how to let go of what they are holding on to, thinking that it is what's keeping them strong, strikes fear in the hearts of most men in prison.

As time went on, I became a Muslim leader for several different camps, teaching a strict form of Islam called Salafi. I saw all Christians as fuel for the hellfire and believed they needed to be saved. As I felt myself growing in influence within the system, my heart was dying from hatred—hatred for a group of people (Christians) who truly loved God and loved people. It took years for me to understand that and for God to open my heart to Jesus Christ. (More on that topic is found in my book *From Darkness to Light*.) At this time, I was in prison with guys old enough to be my father. Because of my ability to work with other groups, the wardens began to rely on me to keep the peace in the prison. To me, it was an opportunity to keep the brothers who considered me their leader safe and to help them go home when it was time. The only problem with this was most wardens fear someone who has too much power. So they would use me and then ship me to another prison.

I remember one warden telling me that the problem was if everyone listened to me when I ask them to do right, what would happen if one day I got mad and asked them to riot? I told her that she should know me better than to think I would push these men to harm themselves and others and destroy their chances of going home. This was the mentality of the gang leaders in prison—to send guys within the gang on missions that would destroy their lives in prison while the leader worked to go home. The warden had promised not to transfer me to another prison, but like all of the other wardens, she shipped me to another location. This left me at a crossroads: should I help people because I want to help them, or should I be quiet and hide within the walls and waste away? I asked myself every morning, "What makes me different from the thousands of inmates who are in prison with me?"

The next morning, I started to do even more to help the young men in prison. In prison, blacks are given details like cooking, cleaning the dorm, picking up paper, washing cars, and other work dealing with sanitation. The white inmates are given the maintenance jobs where they learn skills and work on the inner structure of the prison. This is how you get true hands-on training. For example, at any prison that is almost 85 percent black, you will only find one black guy, if any, on the maintenance team. It is almost like an underlying code that blacks are good for nothing but cleaning the prisons. It's the same way for mobile construction. You wonder why the conditions of people coming out of prison are the way they are. Of course, this is not the only factor. However, it does have a way of weighing heavy on your mind once you start the road to changing your life.

In Smith State Prison, one of the worst prisons in Georgia, I was sitting in the first faith-based dorm ever started there. I came across a Christian brother by the name of Ervin White. As we worked together to help this program move forward, we became great friends. Little did I know that as I studied both the Bible and the Quran, God had a plan for me—a plan much different from what I had planned for myself. Ervin and I came together to create the first mentor program in Georgia's prison system called Young Men on the Move. We involved about eighty lost and angry young men who were getting into trouble. We felt deeply that we could help these young men develop into leaders, that we could teach them to outgrow the gangs and live beyond the title of inmate. Remember, I had found the route to escape prison, so I taught them how to find their way over the fence as well.

Within months, they were on a new path. I knew that these young men—black, white, and Hispanic—would never be offered a job in maintenance. So we created an apprenticeship program that allowed each young man to simply walk with the maintenance crew to learn their daily routine. Now, we told these young men that even though they were only carrying a toolbox, they should pay attention and learn what the crew did and how they did it. Then, when they returned to the dorm, they should play it over and over in their heads. The time would come when they would be asked to do something, and they had to step up and make it happen. I pushed them to be prepared for the opportunity when it presented itself and to not be troubled by the wait, for the knowledge they gained would work toward their success.

What they didn't know was I was going to make sure that they got their chance to show they were worthy of being part of the crew. It was as simple as telling the regular inmates on the maintenance team to get sick. I still held a great deal of power being the Muslim leader at that prison. I gave respect to the smallest of people; therefore, I demanded respect from others. I later learned that the way I lived my life was also a technique taught in the laws of attraction. So it was easy to have the guys on the maintenance team believe in what I was trying to do for these young men. Young Men on the Move was a great success, gaining the praise of wardens and the head chaplain for the Department of Corrections, Mr. Danny Horn.

CHAPTER EIGHT

Bitterness

By this time, I had spent seventeen years in prison. I had been locked up more than half of my life. I was growing from a child into an adult in an environment that was not designed for such a purpose. It was hard to see grown men come to prison with life sentences and make parole in less time than I had spent. It was as if we were forgotten in the system. No one who has been to college and has come home with a degree in criminal studies can tell you what it's like to wake up every morning and look into the black hole of your life. You begin to wonder how your life could become this dark, and you keep looking into the darkness of your day-to-day life in prison.

One morning, while looking into that pit, I saw someone looking back at me. This person was no longer a young man. His eyes had the look of determination, and he showed no fear. That person was me. I was no longer a child. My outer self had caught up to how the world was treating me. I was that adult whom they tried in court as a child. This is the moment that most guys allow bitterness and hatred to enter their heart, which creates a feeling that someone owes me attitude. This feeling is destructive for the inmate and society, not to mention the family. I had to stay focused on the fact that all that I was doing to better myself was not just to make parole; it was done for me and me alone.

The only things I had received from the parole board were two letters explaining that due to the nature of my crime, my parole was denied. After serving the first seven years, I was told that I needed to serve eight more years. After serving fifteen years in prison, I received another letter stating that my parole was denied and I had to serve eight more years. Guys were telling me that I should be mad. They would say that I should stop trying to help everybody and taking all these self-help classes. Being too good was a sign of manipulation. I paid them no mind since my mind was expanding every day, and I needed no papers to say that I could be set free. No bars could hold my mind; no officer could beat the positive thinking out of me. I would tell guys in prison that no officer could outthink me in this environment and that they should feel the same way. We lived this life while they only came to work a job.

CHAPTER NINE

Becoming a Person of Influence

Here is the key to the success within prison: Do not just better yourself for parole. Whatever classes you take, whatever you do to better yourself in prison, it cannot be done so you can make parole. That should never be the goal or motivation. The key is that you work on yourself for yourself. You can't expect or look for family and friends to change how they think about you because you decided to change. When everyone you know sees you as the harsh person who committed a crime, that can't have any effect on your fight to change. Even when prisoners make parole, they cannot live their lives trying to prove to others that they have changed. The only thing they can do is *be* that changed person. Not a day can pass without working on yourself. You can never say, "Now I'm ready for society. Now they should let me go home." Parole was a privilege, not a right. Until then I had work to do on myself, not every month but every day, and not just every day but every second. The key is to be prepared so when the chance comes, you don't waste time trying to get ready and destroy your chance to be free. Many guys would say, "I have ten years to serve. I will start to go to school in my ninth year." Those are self-destructive words for self-destructive thinking.

After serving twenty-three years in prison, I found myself in Rogers State Prison. At this time, cell phones were as easy to get as walking to the bathroom. Underpaid officers had created a black market that would cost you $300 for a prepaid flip phone and $900 to $1,000 for a touch screen. Everyone desired to talk to friends who normally you could not reach in the prison. However, it also allowed gangs to arrange criminal activity from prison to prison and even dorm to dorm. Rogers State Prison was having a real problem with gangs. Some guys were being kidnapped from their dorms and tortured over the weekend in another dormitory. Parents would call about their son being beaten up or bullied. The response from staff was "All your son needs to do is tell us who they are, and we will take care of it." Your son is not going to tell because the staff can't protect him. Gangs would take a picture of your ID card so if you informed staff about them and got transferred for your safety, your picture would be placed on what was known as the most wanted list. It was a blast that sent out a text to over five hundred phones stating that the person in this photo should be beaten on sight. Reward $100, must send proof. A few days later, and sometimes not even a day later, a picture would come across everyone's phone of the guy tied up and beaten.

Gang members would attack the weak, and most of the time the white guys were the weak ones. They were easy targets for young gang members. This led the way for white guys to come together and form white supremacy groups like the Aryan Nation and other white supremacist prison gangs. This existed in prisons in other states but at that time not in the Georgia prison system. So when the white guys started to organize, other inmates wanted the Muslims to put an end to it. I was not angry at them. How else could they survive? Now the playing field was being balanced. Prisons work when the opposing team is just as strong as the team it is up against. This is how you form treaties between gangs. You help the power become equal. I learned there were only two types of people: those who were on the chessboard and those who were moving the pieces on the board. I was determined to be the one moving the pieces.

Because my program was the only one in Georgia's prison system for youth, it had caught the ear of Mr. Stephen Reba, a professor at Emory University's Barton Child Law and Policy Center. I can remember our first visit. He wanted to be sure that all the good things he had heard about me were true. He had heard that I was mentoring young men who had come through the system as I had and that wardens were using me to keep the peace within the prison system. The meeting was the start of a great friendship and the road to my freedom. Even though he said that I had already laid the groundwork, I'm forever grateful for his help in pulling together all that I had done and putting into a package. All the positive things that I had done and the many lives I had touched were scattered. Steve brought it all together, showing how I had grown into a man ready for society.

The warden at Rogers State Prison was named Mr. Hooks. He was one of the very few honest wardens that I met while in prison. I remember being called to his office one day. While being escorted to his office in handcuffs, I was trying to figure out what I had done wrong. When I was pushed into his office, he said, "Take those handcuffs off of him," and he told the officers to leave. The officers did not like that at all. To most of them I was an inmate who had too much power. He knew of all the things that I had been involved in, good and bad, within his institution. But today he wanted to know if his prison was going to be part of the work stoppage that the Georgia inmates were planning to take place that month.

Rogers State Prison was a work prison that supplied most of the prisons in Georgia with canned foods and other things. If that prison shut down, it would be devastating with lasting effects on the other state prisons. We had already been talking on our cell phones about how to start the sit-down. I told the warden to give me a week, and I would have an answer by then. Maybe if most wardens would have taken these steps, those riots would have never happened.

I was given open access to pull all the gang leaders together, along with the Christians who at that time didn't look out for each other as they should have. They spent too much time trying to be holier than the next man. Judgment time was always in session.

I spoke to all of the leaders about the pros and cons of our sit-down and about my experience in situations just like the one we were facing. Telling them what to do would restrict their ability to grow. The pros were, yes, you would make the staff work harder and you would not have to go to work for free. But the outcome of such actions would be a lockdown. All that they had, including their cell phones, would be taken from them, as well as what little freedom they had. I wanted to give them the opportunity to make the right decision. I was determined to lay out the picture for them and allow them to make a choice. Wardens don't appreciate that when you allow people, who have been stripped of the power to choose almost anything, to be given the power to make a choice, it is a positive experience for all those involved. It really helps the inmates to learn and grow. The majority of the time, if the picture is made clear, people will rise to the occasion and make a wise choice.

All of the inmates I spoke with decided to not be a part of the sit-down. Of course, they had a few demands, such as extra TV time and no shakedowns for a week, but nothing too crazy. The next week, I sat in front of Warden Hooks to let him know that his camp would not riot tomorrow. The following day, I was the first one out the door to work. You can't stand for something if you're not willing to be the first to move on it. Actions are what matter most.

CHAPTER TEN

Freedom Is a Choice

After I had served twenty-four years in prison, having been incarcerated since the age of sixteen for a crime committed when I was fifteen, someone from the parole board was coming down to interview me. I prayed all night. However, I did not want to have high hopes for a positive outcome. The higher you fly, the harder you fall. It was just too much of a mental drain to be looking for a positive word from the parole board when there was so much negative living around me. It always seemed that the ones who made parole were the ones who were doing nothing to better themselves in prison. After all of these years, the moment had arrived when I could speak for myself.

I went into the meeting ready for whatever God had for me. My heart was pounding; however, I knew this was and would be my only chance to look someone from the parole board in the face and let them see that I was no longer that lost young man who took a life twenty-four years ago. When I went into the room, the parole officer said, "Well, I just came back from talking to Warden Hooks"—who at that time was the warden over Johnson State Prison—"and he has given you a strong recommendation for parole." I could not believe what I was hearing. Several wardens had told me that they would help me with my parole before. Each one used me to keep the peace and then shipped me away to another facility. I was shocked. Could this really be happening? The parole officer said that he couldn't promise anything, but the possibility looked good. He seemed optimistic. There was hope. I realized that when you do good, others will speak on your behalf. That day I didn't call my family even though I was feeling very positive. I had seen my mother's hopes be beaten down, and she would feel every blow when the parole board sent a letter saying I had to do eight more years. It seemed to age her many years to soon.

I was called to the warden's office the following week. Warden Hooks talked to me like a son. He told me he had children and that his job was to keep them safe by making sure violent offenders stay locked up, and that I should understand that. He went on to say that he had spent twenty-five years working in corrections, and he had only made recommendations for one person to make parole. Now I had become the second person. Warden Hooks gave me great advice. He said, "You've got to let that slickness go. That slick way of doing things that has helped you survive prison will not help you survive in society." He told me that I would only get one chance and one chance alone and that if I came back to prison, I would never see freedom again. And he was right. That advice has stayed with me.

I had essentially grown up in prison. I had seen several of my friends die. One of my friends even died in my arms. I witnessed rapes and guys being stabbed by inmates or beaten by staff. I had held men on my shoulders, trying to keep them up in the air until someone came to cut the rope that they had tied around their neck. I witnessed young men so highly medicated that they struggled to raise a fork to their mouth. One of my close friends was being given a forced shot once a month. That shot would last a month. Once I started to work with his mind and body to get him off the medication, I could see a change in him. I believed in him, and I needed him to believe in himself. When he was asked whom he wanted to speak to the doctors on his behalf, he chose me. Never was another inmate chosen to speak to the doctors at a hearing to determine if a person could stop taking this type of medication. That day was the beginning of a new life for him, a life without medication. I saw officers bring box cutters to white inmates and get them to slice a guy that the officer was having problems with. After the inmate cut the guy, the officer would rush him out of the dorm to protective custody. Over the years, I watched inmates who spent ten to twenty years inside and never received a letter in the mail or made a single phone call. Guys would sell their dinners for an entire week for one cigarette. I knew men who would cut themselves and bleed out just to get away from the pain of doing time.

I remember when I allowed an older inmate, who had been in prison for twenty-nine years, to use my cell phone. He started crying when I gave him the phone. I assumed I had said something wrong, or maybe he thought I would charge him for it. The man looked at me and said, "I don't know how to even turn this on." He reminded me of myself when I was first given a cell phone; I had asked the same question.

I had spent the last twenty-four years in prison not being able to open a refrigerator to get what I wanted. Everything I owned fit on two shelves in a wall locker box. Twenty-four years and I had only seen society through razor fences. So when Warden Hooks said to me, "The Aakeem that lived in this world must be left in this world. If you are going to have any chance of being successful in society, that Aakeem has to die," I knew it was true. I needed to move on in order not to move back. The prison of my past would no longer hold me back from my future.

That year, my body was paroled, and it was about to reunite with my mind, which had escaped from prison many years ago. I was sent to Clayton County Halfway House, which was in a way darker than prison because so many guys were still breaking the law while at the same time not even trying to get a job. It was always someone else's fault why they couldn't find a job. Guys were doing more drugs in the halfway house than in prison. It was like they had no control. It was like a race to see who could get back to their old ways the fastest. Some of the guys had been there over a year and still hadn't found work, but they would tell you that they didn't want to work. These were the guys who left their minds in prison, and their bodies were only halfway out. They were the ones who made it hard for those who were really suffering due to mental health issues or having been abused throughout their life.

Can we reach them? Can we unlock that greatness inside of them? Yes, we can. Too often we speak to the problem but never to the solution. You have to have an attitude that pushes the inner you to become addicted to success. We all have the same potential, a greatness inside of us. For some it takes someone to help them unlock that inner greatness. This unlocking is what I've been teaching men for many years. Once you unlock your relentless attitude, you will prepare to fill out applications years before you come home. You will sit in prison and create mock interviews. You will not wait for your year to be paroled. Every day, every second behind those walls you have to prepare for your freedom no matter how far away that day is. I learned that I had to stop giving myself excuses.

My life was in my hands. I knew that what happened would be a result of my will to make it happen. An Emory Law professor Mr. Steven Reba asked me to address a group of public defenders in downtown Atlanta. My assignment was to help them understand the lawyer-client relationship in order to better help their young clients. That meeting was a success and the start of my journey to be a motivational speaker. The first day that I went out searching for a job, I had shaved and dressed in a suit, looking like a million dollars. Others standing in line with me wore their street clothes, figuring that they wouldn't get a job. My father picked me up. It was strange riding in a car and even stranger riding with my dad after all those years. We didn't know what to say or even how to say it. I could only tell that he was happy to have his son home by the tears in his eyes and the smile on his face. He took me to Wendy's to fill out an application. The manager looked at me and said, "Young man, now you came ready to impress." She gave me an interview right then and hired me on the spot. It had been about twenty-five years now, and on my first day out in society I had found a job. My father was so proud of me. So many people had been telling him how crazy I would be once I came home. Even my father's brother suggested that I get counseling if or when I came home. Little did they understand the transformation that my life had gone through.

If you ask most inmates if they would get a job once they went home, they will say, "No matter what the job is I will do it." That thinking is a time bomb waiting to explode. You can't take care of a family working at a burger place, where kids tell you what to do in disrespectful ways. Soon you will go back to what you know how to do to get money—and that will take you back to prison. If you get the skills in prison, you will not have to settle for anything in society. Yes, my first job was a burger place; however, I never stopped looking. I moved from there to working on cars. I had the skills to do that type of work. Still not satisfied I continued to seek better employment. Many doors were closed in my face. With each closed door, my determination only increased. Remember, I refused to make any excuses for myself while others would say that job was not right for them. I was already moving forward with my life. I had developed a habit of seeing it before I saw it. Seeing myself successful within myself before I saw it around me. My life my journey was not based on what others did that day because I was seeing years down the line of my life.

People say that I'm different or that I'm unique. Yes, my transformation is not the norm. But what is stopping it from becoming the norm, from seeing people come out of prison ready for society, ready to be wives, husbands, fathers, mothers, or just good people? I truly feel that the answer is in using people like me who spent many years behind bars and found a way to redirect their lives and work alongside the state to bring about real change in the prison system.

CHAPTER ELEVEN

When He Touched Me

When I was speaking to youth, I came in contact with a lovely lady named Pamela, who would soon become my wife. We became friends, always debating the Bible. You see, my hatred for those who called themselves Christians was real. It was not so much hatred toward them but toward their belief system. Pamela made it clear that if I was to have a chance with her, I at least had to take a trip to her church. I had no fear of her so-called Jesus. I went to church with her and even sat down to talk with her bishop, Mr. Gibbs. I knew that in a debate he would have no win against the questions I was trained to ask. Bishop Gibbs's demeanor was calm and kind. Every time I said something that I knew would make a Christian upset, he only smiled and said, "I understand, but God stills love you and so do I." I could not understand this type of love. He should have gotten mad and tried to defend what he believed. But he would just smile and say he loved me and that greatness was in me.

Bishop Gibbs wanted to ask one last question after I told him about my life. I said, "Sure, no problem," feeling as if I had won this debate. He said, "You say all Christians are fuel for the hellfire." I said yes. The bishop replied, "Then the very woman who you say you would lay down your life for, Mrs. Collins, is in the hellfire because of her belief." At that moment I felt a pull at my soul. The burden of hatred that I was caring pulled me to my knees. I had become so blinded by the way Christianity was presented to me as a child that I did not see that I had turned my back on the one person who loved me despite my past and denied the root of her love, which was the love of Jesus Christ. That day I realized that while I spent all those years reading the Bible to discredit it, God was planting a seed in my heart.

On my knees in that room, I heard God's voice, and it felt as if the air was being sucked out of the room. He said to me, "You have fought against me most of your life, and I still loved you. Now you fight alongside the truth. You are free, my son." I had rejected the notion of God having any sons, and now I was being called a son by God. I cried out," My God! My God! I surrender unto you." More chains broke away from my mind and my heart. I gave it all to God that day—all my pain, all my hatred, all my desire to fight a holy war and die on the battlefield. My body was set ablaze by His spirit. I knew I needed to be baptized. The next day, on my own and still on fire, I found a local church and was baptized in a little pool. The pastor didn't even know my name. I believe it was the look in my eyes that told him this request needed to be honored. The water cooled me, and God's mission for my life called me.

God started to open doors in my life in a powerful way. It had been three years since I had sent a program up to the Department of Juvenile Justice that would help young men make the step from childhood to adult within the justice system. The proposal was accepted, and I started to work as a contractor for the Department of Juvenile Justice. God pulled on me even more, and in church I could not sit still. I can remember telling my wife, "I have to spread the love of God out into the hurting places of the world." I went to the Georgia School of Ministry and became a minister for the Assemblies of God, reaching out to multiracial crowds with the love of God. My wife and I started to reach out to Muslims, Jehovah's Witnesses, gang members, and those who felt forgotten. I had worshiped a god that I was taught that didn't dwell around us and it was foolish to even believe that he was in us. For years I saw god as far away. When Jesus called my name the understanding that he is right here with us around us and in us God became personal a true relationship was formed.

All those years I had been trapped inside myself, suffering at the hands of how I saw myself and the words that people had spoken over me and into my life. I had locked away the person that God had created me to be. Now, as I minister to people all over the globe, it always is a blessing to introduce people to themselves. God's greatest gift to humankind is not hidden from us; we carry it around with us all our lives. That gift is who God created us to be. Through the relationship with Christ my inner man was set free. However I was still subject to the control of the parole rules. After five years of building a road to success for myself and my family in August 2018 during a DISC certification I received news that made me shout unto God how great He is. I received form the Parole Board a full clemency. That all my rights are restored that from that day I will be no longer be under parole or any other person. God have open a door in my life that men thought was closed. I was completely a free man. I realized at that moment that the message that I was to preach was to the whole human. Not just about the spirit you but the parts of us that are in pain and beaten down by the words in our heads.

CHAPTER TWELVE

True Leadership Adds Value

I remember the books I studied in prison that helped me become a leader, and I remember that the author, John Maxwell, was also a Christian. Those books on leadership saved my life. They kept me from becoming institutionalized and challenged me to grow. I joined the John Maxwell team and became a speaker, coach, and trainer. This was a groundbreaking decision in my life. Through the John Maxwell method I have been able to add value to people in so many ways. I learned from Aaron Antolon, who had become a great friend of mine, that I could also become certified to teach DISC through Personality Insights. In order to become a behavioral consultant, I went on to complete that task while becoming the outreach pastor for the Tabernacle Church. I have been blessed to speak at several schools and institutions, sharing my life story and my pattern for success. The juvenile program that is now called Step to Change has saved lives and families. I, along with Chaplain Danny Horn and the Georgia Department of Juvenile Justice staff, have created the only program of its kind in the United States of America. Step to Change has not only changed lives, but it also has saved lives.

I often wondered why God didn't push my heart toward the love of Christ as a Christian while I was in prison. I no longer ask that question because God has answered it for me. Many people in prison find religion, looking for a "get out of jail" ticket from God. Even some Muslims changed their faith hoping that the Christian organization would help them come home. God said to me that if I had become a Christian in prison before my parole, I would have worshipped Him based on what He did, not who He is. I needed to be a free man and make a free decision to follow Christ. The chains of false beliefs had to be something I was willing to break. Against the odds, against the threats on my life, against my blood becoming lawful to spill, and against losing all the friends I had spent the last twenty-five years with. I had to answer the question from God: "Will you surrender?" So now I ask you the same: Will you surrender to Christ?

Books coming in 2019

Old Wineskin

Stop Feeding the Snakes

For information on bookings for speaking, coaching, training, and DISC training, please contact: Alisa Fields at (646) 271-8852 or Aakeemwoodard@gmail.com.

Feel free to connect: Pastoraakeem@outlook.com

CPSIA information can be obtained
at www.ICGtesting.com
Printed in the USA
FFHW020951050919
54773339-60454FF